ON THE CROSS OF CHRIST

METROPOLITAN YOUSSEF

On the Cross of Christ
By Metropolitan Youssef

Copyright © 2025 Coptic Orthodox Diocese of the Southern U.S.A.

All rights reserved.

Designed & Published by:
St. Mary & St. Moses Abbey Press
101 S Vista Dr, Sandia, TX 78383
stmabbeypress.com

Cover icon was written by the iconographer Gergis Samir.

All Scripture quotations in the footnotes of this book, unless otherwise indicated, are taken from the New King James Version® Copyright © 1982 by Thomas Nelson, Inc. Used by permission. All rights reserved.

Contents

Introduction	5
CHAPTER ONE Bearing My Cross	7
CHAPTER TWO Types of Crosses	12
CHAPTER THREE Through the Cross, God's Attributes are Revealed	22
CHAPTER FOUR The Cross is the Foundation of Our Christian Life	30
CHAPTER FIVE The Ineffable Forgiveness of God	44
CHAPTER SIX Meditations on the Cross	61
CHAPTER SEVEN The Cross & the Eucharist	71
CHAPTER EIGHT The Cross & the Old Testament Offerings	80

"For it is only on the cross that a man dies with his hands spread out. Whence it was fitting for the Lord to bear this also and to spread out His hands, that with the one He might draw the ancient people, and with the other those from the Gentiles, and unite both in Himself."

St. Athanasius the Apostolic

On the Incarnation of the Word 25. (NPNF² 4)

Introduction

The Cross: A Lost-and-Found Treasure

What happened to our beloved holy cross? Has history recorded the holy cross as a lost and forgotten treasure? On the seventeenth day of the blessed month of Thoout, which coincides with September 27th, Orthodox Christians celebrate the Feast Day of the Appearance of the Honorable Cross. St. Helen, a devout Christian queen and the mother of Emperor Constantine, is credited with the discovery of the cross of our Lord Jesus Christ. Can you imagine that a Queen went in search of the blessing of a once spiritless piece of lumber? This only endears to our hearts even more the significance of the holy cross. The story of her search and discovery of the honorable cross is one of enduring perseverance. When she arrived in Jerusalem, she inquired of the Jews in that city about the whereabouts of the holy cross. They would not disclose to her the information she requested, but instead told of an aged Jew named Judas who might assist her. At her persistence, he told her of a pile of dirt and rubbish that the holy cross could be found beneath.

How did this pile of dirt and rubbish come to cover our sacred holy cross? The Jewish leaders in those days, following the crucifixion, when they saw all the signs and wonders made manifest from the holy cross, wished to do away with the holy cross. They commanded all of Judea and Jerusalem to cast the sweepings and dirt from their houses over the holy cross which our Messiah carried to Golgotha after He was condemned to death. Tradition tells us the dirt continued to be placed upon the holy cross for more than two hundred years. How frightened the Jewish leaders must have been of that wooden holy cross!

Queen Helen ordered the immediate removal of the Lord Jesus Christ's holy cross from the trash heap. She then built a church for it and had the church consecrated. The actual appearance of the cross was on the tenth of Paremhotep (March 19th), but because this date is always during fasting, the early church fathers substituted the seventeenth of Thoout, for the Feast of the Cross, which is the date of the consecration of the church in honor of the appearance of the holy cross.

> *"And the wood of the Cross is of saving efficacy for all men, though it is, as I am informed, a piece of a poor tree, less valuable than most trees are."*
>
> ### St. Gregory of Nyssa
>
> *On the Baptism of Christ.* (NPNF[2] 5)

1

Bearing My Cross

The Lord Christ was once walking with a great multitude of people who were following Him. The Lord did not desire that people follow Him without knowing the requirements of becoming followers. What are the requirements of discipleship? He stood and said three conditions that are required to be His disciples.

The first condition is that the Lord should have the priority in our lives, for He said, "If anyone comes to Me and does not hate his father and mother, wife and children, brothers and sisters, yes, and his own life also, he cannot be My disciple."[1] The Lord should have priority; otherwise, we cannot be His disciples. The second condition is that we should carry our own cross, for He said, "And whoever does not bear his cross and come after Me cannot be My disciple."[2] And

---

1 Luke 14:26.
2 Luke 14:27.

the third condition is that the person should forsake being attached to money, and the love of money, and dependence on money; otherwise, they cannot be His disciples, for He said, "Whoever of you does not forsake all that he has cannot be My disciple."[3]

He said to them that they should "sit down first and count the cost."[4] What does counting the cost mean? To follow Me and be My disciples, there are sacrifices you are supposed to offer. Are you able to offer these sacrifices or not? It is like someone who wants to build a building. He will sit down and count the cost. Does he have the amount of money needed to build this building or not? For if he does not have the amount of money, he will begin building, and people will mock him because he cannot finish. Or it is like a king who is going to make war. He will consider whether he can meet the other army with the army he has, or not. If he cannot make war, he will say, "No, I will sign a peace treaty."

He also said to them, "You are the salt of the earth."[5] For you to be a good salt, you must keep these three conditions. If you, however, do not adhere to these conditions, then the salt has lost its flavor, and "if the salt loses its flavor, how shall it be seasoned? It is then good for nothing."[6] The person will be unable to fulfill their mission in the world, to be "the light

---

3   Luke 14:33.
4   Luke 14:28.
5   Matthew 5:13.
6   Ibid.

of the world"[7] and "the salt of the earth."[8] Salt means that the person preserves the world from corruption through their morals, principles, virtues, and attitude. The Lord said to them, "But if the salt has lost its flavor, how shall it be seasoned? It is neither fit for the land nor for the dunghill."[9] The word "dunghill" is derived from the word "dung," that is, the excrement of animals. They used to add salt to the dung to enhance its efficacy as fertilizer. So He is saying that it is not even fit to be used as salt that they mix with the dung, that is, the excrement of animals. "It is then good for nothing."[10]

The Condition of the Cross

Concerning the second condition, the Lord said, "And whoever does not bear his cross and come after Me cannot be My disciple."[11] Why did the Lord place the cross as a condition to becoming followers? He did so because we must suffer and bear the cross, so that we may receive the glory. To inherit the kingdom of heaven, we must be one with Him. Because we are in the Son, we become sons of God, meaning that our sonship to God the Father takes place only when we are united with the Son. If I am separated from the

---

7   Matthew 5:14.
8   Matthew 5:13.
9   Luke 14:34–35.
10 Ibid.
11 Luke 14:27.

Son, then I would have no sonship to God the Father, and would have no inheritance in the kingdom of heaven.

For this reason, my unity with the Son is a fellowship with the Son, fellowship of His sufferings and fellowship of His resurrection and glory, as St. Paul said: "That I may know Him and the power of His resurrection, and the fellowship of His sufferings, being conformed to His death."[12] It is impossible for you to separate yourself from the Son's sufferings and then say that you want to be a partner with Him in the glory. If you are not a partner in the sufferings, you will not be a partner in the glory. The Son endured sufferings for us; He endured all the sufferings and the humiliation and the cross, for my sake, to save me. So, how do I not endure this suffering and become a partner with Him in the suffering?

Therefore, the way to glory has become the way to suffering. St. Paul the Apostle says, "For to you it has been granted on behalf of Christ, not only to believe in Him, but also to suffer for His sake."[13] It is now a gift that we unite with the Son in suffering. And the Lord, out of His love, has made suffering a reason for blessing. In this manner, the cross is now a reason for blessing, but the cross before Christ was a sign of shame, disgrace, and humiliation, and was a curse. Now, the cross is a sign of pride and glory, and it

---

12   Philippians 3:10.
13   Philippians 1:29.

has power. The demons are terrified by the sign of the cross. For this reason, the Lord said that we cannot be His disciples, be one with Him, and inherit the glory, while we refuse to bear the cross.

> *"Let us accept anything for the Word's sake. By sufferings let us imitate His Passion: by our blood let us reverence His Blood: let us gladly mount upon the Cross. Sweet are the nails, though they be very painful. For to suffer with Christ and for Christ is better than a life of ease with others."*
>
> **St. Gregory Nazianzus**
>
> *The Second Oration on Easter* XXIII. (NPNF[2] 7)

2

Types of Crosses

There are many crosses that a person faces in their life. Some crosses come upon us from outside, and there are other crosses that we choose for ourselves, and we go into these by our own free will.

Crosses That Come from Outside

An example of the crosses that come upon us from outside is the cross of persecution. People who hate Christ and Christians rise and persecute them. And the Church has been persecuted since the days of our Lord Jesus Christ. After He was born, the children of Bethlehem were killed. Christ was persecuted throughout His life. The religious leaders of the Jews wanted to kill Christ, and in the end, they crucified Him. And after Christ's crucifixion and resurrection, they persecuted the Apostles. All the Apostles, except John, were killed and martyred. And the persecution of the Church continued to be intense, and the blood of millions of martyrs was shed for the name of Christ, until King Constantine came and ended the persecution. But did the persecution actually end? No, it did not end.

After that came the Council of Chalcedon, in which the Church was divided on the subject of whether Christ has one nature or two natures. Those who agreed with the Council of Chalcedon were the ones who believed in the two natures of Christ. And they began to persecute the miaphysites,[14] that is, us. And the persecution was fierce, and they tortured and killed people. We call those who were tortured but did not die confessors, for example, Abba Samuel the Confessor. It was the Chalcedonians who plucked his eye out because he refused to sign the Tome of Leo, which stated that Christ has two natures.

Afterwards came the persecution of the Church by the Arabs, and until today, the Church has been persecuted. And the persecution takes various forms. It may take the form of killing and torturing, but it may take another form, that is, leading the people astray from the truth. Nowadays, they cause people to doubt the Lord. If you do not believe in the principles of the world, you find yourself persecuted and treated differently. If you say that you believe in the existence of God, and those around you are atheists, you are treated differently. If you say that you do not believe

---

14 I.e. those who believe that Christ has one nature out of two natures.

in same-sex marriage, transgenderism, and abortion, they persecute you, treat you differently, and tell you that you are a fanatic.

The Church is still persecuted until today. The word of truth is rejected. See, for example, the Feast of Nativity. It is forbidden in many places to mention the word "Christ." It is difficult to find a Christmas card with a picture of Christ. This is one of the kinds of persecution. They turned Christmas into a tree and Santa Claus, and that is it, completely removing Christ. Behind all the excitement of Christmas is business, to sell gifts and make money. Consider also the Feast of the Resurrection. Try to feel it. The Feast of the Resurrection is very weak, and you do not feel it here [in the West]. They either make very minor celebrations for it or not at all. They turned it into rabbits, because the feast of fertility is in the spring.

Christianity is persecuted. It is a cross to say that you are a Christian. It is a cross to be a stranger in the world. The Lord said, "If you were of the world, the world would love its own. Yet because you are not of the world, but I chose you out of the world, therefore the world hates you."[15] Because we are not of the world, the world hates us. There are some people who begin to grow weak, others who begin to flatter, and yet others who sacrifice their principles, all this so that they may be accepted in the world. But in this manner, you are not bearing your cross, and the Lord

---

15 John 15:19.

said, "And whoever does not bear his cross and come after Me cannot be My disciple."[16]

Bearing the cross means that I hold on to my Christianity and defend my faith and my religion, no matter what the cost is. And I say, "Yes, we are Christians. We believe in the existence of God. We believe in the incarnation of His only begotten Son and His resurrection." Also, I say, "Same-sex marriage is a sin, a perversion. And the Holy Scripture condemns it. Also, we do not believe in transgenderism and abortion." We must declare these principles strongly and courageously. This is our Christianity. This is the cross, even if the world rejects and renounces us. We are not of the world.

Crosses That Come from Oneself

Sometimes a person chooses by themselves to bear a cross. This is what we call the narrow gate. When our Lord said, "Enter by the narrow gate,"[17] this means that the person chooses to constrain themselves. We read in the Synaxarion, for example, about Luke the Stylite. Someone builds a column, builds a cell on top of this column, and goes up and lives in it, to never come down again. He spends all his life on top of this column, never coming down. Why did he do this? He chose to constrain himself in this way. There is also Simeon the Stylite and others who lived in this way.

---

16   Luke 14:27.
17   Matthew 7:13.

The Cross of Asceticism

You might find someone who is committed to their canon and prayers, but someone else might struggle more with their spiritual canon. For example, they might ask for more prayers; or instead of praying the Midnight Hour at nine p.m., they wake up at three in the morning to pray the Midnight Hour. But you might say, "But how! The person has work the day after." This is one of the kinds of struggles. The person struggles and constrains themselves, entering by the narrow gate. They are not content with praying only, but they struggle more in prayer.

Take fasting, for example. You find in the Nativity Fast that people eat the best types of food. Then someone comes and says that they will constrain themselves in this fast. They will only eat certain kinds of food and stay away from many other kinds that they love. Of course, all of this is done through the guidance of the father of confession. This kind of entering by the narrow gate or bearing the cross, we may call it the cross of asceticism or the cross of being forceful in the spiritual struggle

The Cross of Fleeing from Honor

This means that no sooner does someone find that there is honor than he flees from it. Abba Isaac said, "Honor flees away from before the man that runs after it; but he who flees from it, the same will it hunt down."[18] This is why we read in the lives of the saints that when someone was chosen for the patriarchate or the bishopric, he would run away, because he did not want the honor associated with the patriarchate or the bishopric.

The Virgin St. Mary went and served Elizabeth for three months, and just before John the Baptist was born, she left, because many visitors would sit with Elizabeth during this period. Why did she leave? She left because she did not want to receive honor from the people who would honor her and praise her for serving Elizabeth for three months. There is someone who might speak about himself so that people might praise him, while another, as soon as people praise him, changes the conversation and runs away from the honor.

The Cross of Taking the Last Place and of Laboring in the Service

The person here is content, as the Lord said, "If anyone desires to be first, he shall be last of all and servant of all."[19] This person is truly the last of all and a servant of all joyfully. They are glad when they are last. But sometimes you find that a person becomes troubled if they are not the first, for example, if they are not selected to be on the church committee, or

---

18 *The Ascetical Homilies of Saint Isaac the Syrian.* (Boston, MA: Holy Transfiguration Monastery, 2011), 166.
19 Mark 9:35.

are not made a church servant, or are not chosen as a steward of the service. Someone else, on the other hand, runs away and wants to live in the last place for their whole life, like John the Baptist when He said about the Lord Jesus Christ, "He must increase, but I must decrease."[20]

Some people labor for the sake of serving others. When they hear that someone is sick, they quickly visit him and see if he needs anything, and they get it for him. When they hear that someone is in prison, they run to obtain permission to visit him and ask about him. When they hear that someone has just arrived from Egypt and is trying to settle down, they labor with him, and see what he needs, how to finish his paperwork, how to help him settle, and find a job for him. They love to serve and labor in the service. This is the cross of laboring in the service, which gladdens the heart of the Lord. "If anyone desires to be first, he shall be last of all and servant of all."[21]

The Cross of Renunciation

This is the cross of abandoning something for the sake of the Lord, like how our fathers, the monks, abandoned their wealth and their jobs, abandoning all of this for the sake of the Lord. Abba Anthony was a wealthy young man who inherited 300 acres of land. He abandoned all of it, distributed his money among

---

20 John 3:30.
21 Mark 9:35.

the poor, and went and lived in the desert where he was unknown. He abandoned for the sake of God; this is the cross of renunciation. On the other hand, we sometimes say, "This is my right!" What am I ready to abandon for the sake of the Lord? Which rights am I ready to abandon for the sake of the Lord Jesus Christ? Concerning Him, St. Paul said, "Though He was rich, yet for your sakes He became poor."[22] And the Lord Himself said, "The Son of Man has nowhere to lay His head."[23]

The Cross of Forbearance

St. Paul said, "Bearing with one another in love."[24] Nowadays, no one can endure anyone. For this reason, the cases of divorce have greatly increased. What is the difference between our generation and the two generations before us? We did not hear of such divorces in the forties, fifties, and sixties. Why, nowadays, do people get married, and a couple of years after, they get divorced? What has happened? No one wants to endure and be patient. Where is the ability to bear with one another in love? It no longer exists, because our ego has become inflated.

Where is the cross of forgiveness that a person forgives? When people are upset at each other, it takes months for them to forgive and be reconciled, and

---

22   2 Corinthians 8:9.

23   Matthew 8:20.

24   Ephesians 4:2.

sometimes this happens in one family, a sibling with other siblings, and a father with his children. This is the narrow gate, that I give up my right, that I forgive, saying, "May God forgive you," and that I forget from my heart.

Where are all these principles? No one wants to bear a cross for the sake of our Lord. Yet the Lord says, "And whoever does not bear his cross and come after Me cannot be My disciple."[25] I wonder about our choice today. Do we choose to bear the cross and partake of the sufferings of Christ, so that we may partake of the glory? Or, do we desire to never carry a cross? We do not want to labor; we do not want to endure; we do not want to constrain ourselves. Rather, we want to walk in the broad way. What will you choose for yourself? If you choose the wide gate and the broad way, their end is sadly destruction.[26]

Will you, however, choose to bear the cross and walk behind your Master, He who for your sake endured shame and humiliation, who for your sake was born in a manger, who for your sake fled to the land of Egypt while a young child because Herod wanted to kill Him, who for your sake lived all His life having nowhere to lay His head, who for your sake was humiliated and reviled and spat upon and scourged, who for your sake stood as a criminal before those who judged Him, who for your sake was crucified between

---

25   Luke 14:27.
26   See Matthew 7:13.

two criminals, who for your sake endured all these while He is holy and righteous? Is it too much for me to bear the cross with Him so that I may inherit the kingdom of heaven? "Whoever does not bear his cross and come after Me cannot be My disciple."[27]

> *"If you are a Simon of Cyrene, take up the Cross and follow. If you are crucified with Him as a robber, acknowledge God as a penitent robber. If even He was numbered among the transgressors for you and your sin, do become law-abiding for His sake. Worship Him Who was hanged for you, even if you yourself are hanging."*
>
> ## St. Gregory Nazianzus
>
> *The Second Oration on Easter* XXIV. (NPNF[2] 7)

---

27 Luke 14:27.

3

Through the Cross, God's Attributes are Revealed

Let us reflect upon the cross, and as we do so, a lot of powerful revelations concerning the nature of God will begin to unfold to us.

1. The Power of God

> For the message of the cross is foolishness to those who are perishing, but to us who are being saved it is the power of God.[28]

Every time we look at the cross, it brings to our mind the might and ultimate power that God has. The Holy Bible records incidents of how powerful Satan could get; for example, he was able to hinder

---

28 1 Corinthians 1:18.

Archangel Gabriel from delivering a message to Daniel the prophet, to the extent that Archangel Gabriel had to call upon Archangel Michael to help him deliver the message:

> Then he said to me, "Do not fear, Daniel, for from the first day that you set your heart to understand, and to humble yourself before your God, your words were heard; and I have come because of your words. But the prince of the kingdom of Persia withstood me twenty-one days; and behold, Michael, one of the chief princes, came to help me, for I had been left alone there with the kings of Persia."[29]

The only One that could defeat Satan is our Lord Jesus Christ with the cross, crushing him under His feet and stripping him of all power and dominion: "Having disarmed principalities and powers, He made a public spectacle of them, triumphing over them in it."[30]

In addition, our Lord Jesus Christ granted His followers the same power to defeat Satan with the same means, which is the sign of the cross. Thus, Satan will remain defeated forever as long as we keep this powerful tool before us. And every time Satan launches his attacks through evil thoughts and temptations, we should be able to defeat him with the sign of the cross, reminding him of his utter annihilation in the battle

---

29 Daniel 10:12–13.

30 Colossians 2:15.

that took place at Calvary, and how our Lord was able to bind him and limit his authority.

2. The Holiness of God

> For such a High Priest was fitting for us, who is holy, harmless, undefiled, separate from sinners, and has become higher than the heavens; who does not need daily, as those high priests, to offer up sacrifices, first for His own sins and then for the people's, for this He did once for all when He offered up Himself.[31]

Here, St. Paul is telling us that our Lord was a holy Sacrifice, undefiled, able to save us. Since our sin was against God, to atone for it, salvation could not have been fulfilled except by a Holy One, without blemish and sin.

As we pray in the Divine Liturgy of St. Gregory, "Neither an angel nor an archangel, neither a patriarch nor a prophet, have You entrusted with our salvation, but You, without change, were incarnate and became man, and resembled us in everything, except for sin alone." Every time we look at the cross, we remember the holiness of God, for "in all their affliction He was afflicted, and the Angel of His Presence saved them; in His love and in His pity He redeemed them; and He bore them and carried them all the days of old."[32]

---

31 Hebrews 7:26–27.
32 Isaiah 63:9.

St. Peter, in his first epistle, urges us to conduct our lives in a holy way, "because it is written, 'Be holy, for I am holy,'"[33] to gain fellowship with Him. This explains further why, during the trial of our Lord Jesus Christ, our Lord said to the one who slapped Him, "Why do you strike Me?"[34] One might think that this saying contradicts our Lord's teaching of turning the other cheek. However, it does not, because during the trial our Lord had to defend Himself against the accusation of breaking the Law. But when the soldiers started slapping Him, He neglected His cheeks to those who smite.

Under those circumstances, our Lord was before a double-fold task: that of proving He is a holy Sacrifice without blemish or sin, for His sacrifice to be accepted, and that of implementing His own teaching of leaving His cheeks to the soldiers to be smitten after the trial.

3. The Wisdom of God

But we preach Christ crucified, to the Jews a stumbling block and to the Greeks foolishness, but to those who are called, both Jews and Greeks, Christ the power of God and the wisdom of God. Because the foolishness of God is wiser than men, and the weakness of God is stronger than men.[35]

---

33 1 Peter 1:16.
34 John 18:23.
35 1 Corinthians 1:23–25.

Israel was waiting for an earthly king. However, when the Lord declared that His kingdom is not of this world, they were stumbled. On Hosanna Sunday, they greeted Him with palms, shouting, "This is the King of Israel." But when He went into the temple and preached about His kingdom, they refused Him and ended up crucifying Him on Friday. This way, they had proved that they did not comprehend the wisdom of God, that through the cross, He would become a heavenly King and not an earthly one.

Although the Greeks were well known for their intellect and philosophy, their minds could not understand the mystery of the cross, nor the wisdom of God, thus considering the incarnation and the crucifixion foolishness. What we perceive as foolishness is actually wiser than our wisdom, and the weakness of God is stronger than men. Whenever God does not make sense to us, we turn to our wisdom and intelligence and start to rely on them, and then gradually we convince ourselves of the credibility of our intellect as a sole source of wisdom, and so the wisdom of God becomes mere foolishness in our sight.

That is why a lot of God's commandments do not make much sense to us at the time being until we start to apply them. For example, in the matter of tithing, our human reasoning will never be able to comprehend how, after paying the 10%, the 90% will be more than 100%.

For the same reason, St. Peter was not ready to allow our Lord to wash his feet because he could not understand how the Master would wash the feet of a servant. However, our Lord came up with the right answer in the right context: "What I am doing you do not understand now, but you will know after this."[36]

Under the same precept and in an attempt to subject God's mind to their human understanding, many denominations have shunned the early Church teachings concerning the doctrines. So to them, the Holy Eucharist is not the real Body and Blood of our Lord Jesus Christ but only a symbolic commemoration of them. This is because, despite all the biblical proofs, especially the Gospel of St. John 6, and 1 Corinthians 11, they still cannot comprehend with their mind how the bread and wine, through the descent of the Holy Spirit, are changed to the Body and Blood of Christ. How true is the proverb that says, "Lean not on your own understanding.... Do not be wise in your own eyes."[37]

4. The Humility of God

Let this mind be in you which was also in Christ Jesus, who, being in the form of God, did not consider it robbery to be equal with God, but made Himself of no reputation, taking the form of a bondservant, and coming

---

36 John 13:7.
37 Proverbs 3:5, 7.

in the likeness of men. And being found in appearance as a man, He humbled Himself and became obedient to the point of death, even the death of the cross.[38]

Thus, St. Paul exhorts us to acquire the same humble mind of our Lord Jesus Christ. When we look at the cross, we remember God's greatness shrouded in humility. The sin of Adam and Eve was a sin of pride since they wanted to exalt themselves. That is why humility is the only remedy to pride, and it was only through His humility that our Lord was able to save us and crush Satan. Such lowliness confused Satan; so much so that he kept asking the same question: "If you are the Son of God…" He could not comprehend the language of humility and how God could become a man. Satan's pride created confusion in his mind, disabling him from understanding the mystery of humility, which is the mystery of the cross. When we acquire humility and lowliness of spirit, and accept to decrease, letting others increase, we will then be able to defeat Satan and escape his traps.

St. Paul says that if we humble ourselves before God, He will exalt us and give us a name above all names: "Therefore God also has highly exalted Him and given Him the name which is above every name."[39]

The first daughter of humility is obedience. If we

---

[38] Philippians 2:5–8.
[39] Philippians 2:9.

are stubborn, arrogant, and opinionated, all these being signs of disobedience and pride, we will not be able to attain salvation. The Bible teaches us, saying, "God resists the proud, but gives grace to the humble."[40]

> *"O the divine mystery of that cross, on which weakness hangs, might is free, vices are nailed, and triumphal trophies raised.... Therefore do you also crucify sin, that you may die to sin; he who dies to sin lives to God."*
>
> ### St. Ambrose of Milan
>
> *On the Holy Spirit* I.IX.108–109. (NPNF² 10)

---

40 James 4:6.

4

The Cross is the Foundation of Our Christian Life

1. The Cross is the Foundation of Our Fellowship with God

What do I mean by fellowship with God? In the epistle to the Hebrews, St. Paul said:

> Seeing then that we have a great High Priest who has passed through the heavens, Jesus the Son of God, let us hold fast our confession. For we do not have a High Priest who cannot sympathize with our weaknesses, but was in all points tempted as we are, yet without sin. Let us therefore come boldly to the throne of grace, that we may obtain mercy and find grace to help in time of need.[41]

---

41 Hebrews 4:14–16.

St. Paul is saying that Christ resembled us in everything, even in temptation, yet without sin. So He sympathizes with us. Because I know my God, that He understands me and can sympathize with me, this is why I am not reluctant, I am not shaken, I am not hesitant to approach the throne of God. Rather, I can go boldly to the throne of grace. This boldness we received from the cross of our Lord Jesus Christ, because He resembled us. So we can come boldly to the throne of grace that we may obtain mercy and find grace to help us in time of need. If you are in need, do not be reluctant. Do not say, "God does not love me." Do not say, "God does not accept me." No. The cross is the foundation of our fellowship with God.

St. Paul emphasizes this again in his epistle to the Hebrews, saying:

> Therefore, brethren, having boldness to enter the Holiest by the blood of Jesus, by a new and living way which He consecrated for us, through the veil, that is, His flesh, and having a High Priest over the house of God, let us draw near with a true heart in full assurance of faith.[42]

How do we have this boldness? "By the blood of Jesus," because His blood opens the way—"by a new and living way, which He consecrated for us through the veil," that is, His flesh. So St. Paul is saying that

---

[42] Hebrews 10:19–22.

the blood of Jesus makes me able to approach the throne of God with boldness. This boldness is not based on my worthiness, not because I am worthy, but because Jesus opened the door for me through the veil. He consecrated a new and living way by His blood, so now I can approach the throne of God with boldness.

One of the beautiful verses that again speaks about our boldness is in the epistle to the Romans. Someone might ask, "Who is dearest to the heart of God the Father?" No one is dearest to the heart of God the Father more than His Son, but St. Paul says, "He (God the Father) who did not spare His own Son, but delivered Him up for us all, how shall He not with Him also freely give us all things?"[43] At all times, Satan is telling us, "God does not love you. God does not accept you. Think about your sins. You are not accepted, but are rejected." But St. Paul said, "No. Do you want to know how much God loves you? He did not spare His own Son, but delivered Him up on the cross. How shall He not with Him also freely give us all things?" So now I can approach Christ, I can approach God the Father, the throne of grace with boldness, based on the blood of the Lord Jesus Christ. This is why the cross is the foundation of our fellowship with God the Father. I can approach God the Father. I am no longer an enemy but rather His son.

43　Romans 8:32. Words in parentheses are added for clarification.

2. The Cross is the Foundation of Our Reconciliation and Peace with God

The cross is the foundation of our reconciliation with God and of our peace with God. When we transgressed the commandment of God, we became His enemies, because there is no fellowship between light and darkness. But in the epistle to the Romans, St. Paul says, "Therefore, having been justified by faith, we have peace with God through our Lord Jesus Christ."[44] As I explained, we are already justified by the blood of our Lord Jesus Christ. If we believe in Him, if we accept Him as our Lord and our Savior, we now have peace with God through our Lord Jesus Christ, because we are justified, and all the charges against us are dropped. We are no longer enemies, but rather we are at peace. We are reconciled with Him.

In the Old Testament, when they worshiped, they worshiped facing west. Why? The entrance of the tabernacle of meeting was on the east side, and the Holy of holies was on the west side. Because the Garden of Eden was in the east, when Adam and Eve were expelled from the garden, they were as if giving their back to the east, to the Garden of Eden, and were facing west. So, in all the worship in the Old Testament, people were facing west as a constant reminder that they were not at peace with God. They are enemies to God. They are giving their back to God.

---

44 Romans 5:1.

But now, after having been reconciled with God, we face east in worship. We face Paradise. We are not expelled. Paradise is opened, and all of us have a promise from God that, as He told us, "Do not fear, little flock, for it is your Father's good pleasure to give you the kingdom."[45] Also, in the epistle to the Ephesians, St. Paul says, "For He Himself is our peace, who has made both one, and has broken down the middle wall of separation."[46] Who are the "both"? The Jews and the Gentiles. In the Old Testament, the Gentiles were not allowed to enter the tabernacle of meeting nor the temple. There was a court outside. It was called the court of the Gentiles. So there was a wall separating the Jews from the non-Jewish people, the Gentiles. But now, through the cross, Christ made peace, as St. Paul said. He also said in the same epistle, "But now in Christ Jesus you who once were far off have been brought near by the blood of Christ."[47] By the blood of Christ, you are brought near. You are not outside, in the outer court, but you became one.

What is the middle wall of separation? "Having abolished in His flesh the enmity, that is, the law of commandments contained in ordinances, so as to create in Himself one new man from the two, thus making peace."[48] So He is creating in Himself one new man, in the body of Christ. If I am Jewish, I will join

---

[45] Luke 12:32.
[46] Ephesians 2:14.
[47] Ephesians 2:13.
[48] Ephesians 2:15.

the body of Christ. If I am a Gentile, I am a member of the body of Christ. So, in His body, He made the two one, creating in Himself one new man from the two, thus making peace.

And then He took the two, "that He might reconcile them both to God in one body through the cross, thereby putting to death the enmity."[49] Do you see the beauty? God made the Jews and the Gentiles one in His body, but He is the Son of God; He is one with God. So these two, He reconciled both to God in one body through the cross, thereby putting to death the enmity.

Yes, the cross is the foundation of peace and reconciliation. He reconciled man with himself, man with his brother, and man with God. This is why St. Paul continues, saying, "And He came and preached peace to you who were afar off and to those who were near."[50] "Far off," that is, the Gentiles. "Near," that is, the Jews. "For through Him we both (Gentiles and Jews) have access by one Spirit (Whom we receive in the Sacrament of Chrismation) to the Father. Now, therefore, you are no longer strangers and foreigners, but fellow citizens with the saints and members of the household of God."[51] So yes, in the cross, when we see the cross, we see the peace, peace with myself, peace with my brother, and peace with God. The cross is the foundation of peace.

---

49 Ephesians 2:16.

50 Ephesians 2:17.

51 Ephesians 2:18–19. Words in parentheses are added for clarification.

3. The Cross is the Foundation of Our Forgiveness and Justification

How are we forgiven and justified? Justified means all the charges against us are dropped. When God looks at us, He will say, "You are justified. No charges are against you." In the epistle to the Ephesians, St. Paul says, "In Him we have redemption through His blood, the forgiveness of sins, according to the riches of His grace."[52] Forgiveness of sins, how? Through His blood that was shed on the cross. And we have His Blood every day on the altar. When the Lord Jesus Christ shed His blood on the cross, He kept It for us every day on the altar to drink from His Blood and receive forgiveness of sins. This is not because we are worthy, but it is, as St. Paul said, according to the riches of His grace.

In the epistle to the Romans, we read the same meaning, "Much more then, having now been justified by His blood, we shall be saved from wrath through Him."[53] So, if we are not justified, we will be the object of the wrath of God because of our transgressions and our sins. This is why St. Paul is telling us, "When I am speaking about your justification, you should know that through this justification, you are saved from the wrath of God." And how are we justified? By His blood that was shed on the cross.

---

52 Ephesians 1:7.
53 Romans 5:9.

Also, we know from the epistle to the Hebrews that there is no forgiveness except by blood. As we read, "And according to the law almost all things are purified with blood, and without shedding of blood there is no remission."[54] If the Lord Jesus Christ did not shed His blood on the cross, then we would not be forgiven. So the remission of sins came through the shedding of the blood of our Lord Jesus Christ.

Blood has a meaning of death and life. This is because of how we get the blood. If we kill somebody, shedding his blood, he dies. But if somebody is dying and you transfer the blood to him, he will live. Also, after Cain killed his brother, Abel, the Lord said to Cain, "The voice of your brother's blood cries out to Me from the ground."[55] So if the blood is crying out, then the blood has the characteristic of life.

And St. Paul, in the epistle to the Hebrews, confirms what the Lord said to Cain when he spoke about the blood of our Lord Jesus Christ, saying, "But you have come ... to Jesus the Mediator of the new covenant, and to the blood of sprinkling that speaks better things than that of Abel."[56] Why better things? The blood of Abel was shouting to God, saying, "Avenge me from my brother Cain, who killed me!" So, the blood of Abel was seeking revenge, seeking punishment for Cain. But the blood of Jesus is shouting and crying out, saying, "Forgive them!

---

54 Hebrews 9:22.

55 Genesis 3:10.

56 Hebrews 12:22, 24.

Forgive them!" What a big difference. Blood is asking for revenge, and blood is asking for justification and remission of sins. But if the blood speaks, then the blood here is life.

And we can see how the blood has these two aspects of death and life at the same time in the sacrifices of the Old Testament. In the Old Testament, when a person sinned, he used to bring a sacrifice. And then he would kill the sacrifice, so there is death here. Then the priest takes this blood and sprinkles it on the altar. And once he sprinkles it on the altar, he declares to the person who brought the sacrifice that his sins are forgiven. And when he says that his sins are forgiven, then the charge or the sentence of death against this person is dropped. So here we can see a sacrifice has been killed (death) and a person has been saved—death and life.

Also, on the great Day of Atonement, the Day of Kippur, about which you may read in the sixteenth chapter of Leviticus, the high priest kills the sacrifice. This is death. Then he takes the blood of the sacrifice and enters the Holy of holies. And this was the only time in the year when the priest entered the Holy of holies. And then he sprinkles this blood on the mercy seat. And when he sprinkles the blood on the mercy seat, the seat of mercy, we see mercy and justice meeting each other. Justice by killing the sacrifice, mercy by sprinkling the blood on the mercy seat. Then there is atonement, forgiveness, and justification for everybody.

And we can see how St. Paul put death and life together in the epistle to the Romans when he said about the Lord Jesus Christ, "[Jesus] who was delivered up because of our offenses, and was raised because of our justification."[57] So He died because of our sins. Then He rose and gave us life for our justification. This is why the Lord Jesus Christ, when He gave His Blood in Communion to the disciples, told them, "Drink from it, all of you. For this is My blood of the new covenant, which is shed for many for the remission of sins."[58]

That is why we cannot separate the crucifixion from the resurrection. Crucifixion is death; resurrection is life. This is because if Jesus Christ died and did not rise, as St. Paul said, "We are of all men the most pitiable."[59] We cannot separate death from life, nor can we separate His crucifixion from His resurrection. This is why St. Paul again puts death and life together, in his epistle to the Hebrews, saying, "Now may the God of peace who brought up our Lord Jesus from the dead, that great Shepherd of the sheep, through the blood of the everlasting covenant."[60] It is the covenant of life, justification for us based on the blood of our Lord Jesus Christ. And as the high priest used to enter the Holy of holies once a year, our Lord Jesus Christ entered the Heaven of heavens and the Holy of holies,

---

[57] Romans 4:25.
[58] Matthew 26:27–28.
[59] 1 Corinthians 15:19.
[60] Hebrews 13:20.

not without blood, but with His own blood. He entered the Holy of holies when He ascended into the heavens, and He found eternal redemption for all of us, eternal redemption as St. Paul said in his epistle to the Hebrews: "Not with the blood of goats and calves, but with His own blood He entered the Most Holy Place once for all, having obtained eternal redemption."[61] So when we venerate the cross and when we see the sign of the cross, we remember that the cross of our Lord Jesus Christ is the foundation of our forgiveness, our remission of sins, and our justification. This is why we venerate the cross of our Lord Jesus Christ.

4. The Cross is the Foundation of the Dual Death

What do I mean by dual death? In his epistle to the Galatians, St. Paul said, "But God forbid that I should boast except in the cross of our Lord Jesus Christ, by whom the world has been crucified to me, and I to the world."[62] Focus here on "by whom the world has been crucified to me," so the world is dead to me, "and I to the world." This is what I mean by dual death: I am dead to the world, and the world also is dead to me.

Why is this important? If there is a dead person here, and we brought in front of him all the pleasures of the world, can the pleasures move this dead person? Of course not. So if I am dead to the world, I will not

---

61 Hebrews 9:12.
62 Galatians 6:14.

desire anything from the world because the pleasures of the world cannot move anything in me. This is regarding being dead to the world. On the other hand, the world is dead to me. When something is dead, nobody desires it. So if the world is dead to me, I will not desire anything in the world. So the world cannot move me to desire anything, and I do not desire anything from the world. This is the dual death when he said, "The world is dead to me, and I to the world."

Some people in the Old Testament understood the mystery of the cross prophetically, and they understood the duality of death here, how I am dead to the world, and the world to me. St. Paul mentioned this in his epistle to the Hebrews when he spoke about Moses, saying:

> By faith Moses, when he became of age, refused to be called the son of Pharaoh's daughter, choosing rather to suffer affliction with the people of God than to enjoy the passing pleasures of sin, esteeming the reproach of Christ greater riches than the treasures in Egypt; for he looked to the reward.[63]

He refused to be called the son of Pharaoh's daughter, meaning the palace of Pharaoh was dead to Moses. He did not desire anything of it. Prophetically, Moses, rather, before Christ, accepted to suffer affliction with the people of God, with the reproach

---

63   Hebrews 11:24–26.

of Christ, that is, the cross. Why? "For he looked to the reward." In the cross, we do not desire anything of the passing pleasures of sin. So I am dead to the world, and the world is dead to me.

In the epistle to the Galatians, St. Paul says, "I have been crucified with Christ; it is no longer I who live, but Christ lives in me."[64] If we truly belong to Christ, as we read in the epistle to the Galatians, we should crucify our bodies with Christ. St. Paul says, "And those who are Christ's have crucified the flesh with its passions and desires."[65] This is a dual death. I am dead to the world, and the world is dead to me.

5. The Cross is the Foundation of Our Salvation

> Therefore we must give the more earnest heed to the things we have heard, lest we drift away. For if the word spoken through angels proved steadfast, and every transgression and disobedience received a just reward, how shall we escape if we neglect so great a salvation, which at the first began to be spoken by the Lord, and was confirmed to us by those who heard Him.[66]

---

64 Galatians 2:20.
65 Galatians 5:24.
66 Hebrews 2:1–3.

Every time we look at the cross, we remember what our Lord had to endure to grant us salvation. Salvation is a free gift from God to us, and the main purpose of the incarnation was for our Lord to save us. He became Man, suffered, shed His blood, and died on the cross, only to save us. We sometimes find it hard to labor, strive, and fight against sin to maintain this salvation. However, every time we fall away through sin, we need to return and go back to the Lord and receive this free gift of salvation from Him. In the Divine Liturgy, we pray, "[He] taught us the ways of salvation."[67] We have to utilize the means and go through the channels of Baptism, Repentance, and Communion to be worthy of accepting this free gift.

> *"For the cross destroyed the enmity of God towards man, brought about the reconciliation, made the earth Heaven, associated men with angels, pulled down the citadel of death, unstrung the force of the devil, extinguished the power of sin, delivered the world from error, brought back the truth, expelled the Demons, destroyed temples, overturned altars, suppressed the sacrificial offering, implanted virtue, founded the Churches."*
>
> ### St. John Chrysostom
>
> *Against Marcionists and Manichæans* 2. (NPNF[1] 9)

---

67 The Divine Liturgy of St. Basil – Holy.

5

The Ineffable Forgiveness of God

One of the meanings of the cross is forgiveness. God, on the cross, prayed for the forgiveness of even those who crucified Him and asked the Father not to hold them accountable. We can see that His forgiveness is unconditional, limitless, and willful. On the cross, He made a choice and a decision to forgive all sins of all people, throughout all time. And He said to His disciples, "Drink from it, all of you. For this is My blood of the new covenant, which is shed for many for the remission of sins."[68]

Some might ask, "If God has forgiven all sins of all people, throughout all times, why will some people not be saved although their sins were forgiven?" Because they refuse to receive this gift of forgiveness. So the

---

68 Matthew 26:27–28.

gift of forgiveness is available to everyone in the world, to everyone from Adam to the end of the ages, to every single person. But it depends on us whether we choose this gift of forgiveness or not. Those who choose the gift of forgiveness, to receive it, are reconciled with God. But those who reject the gift of forgiveness are not reconciled with God.

So what does it mean for me to carry my cross and follow Christ? It means to forgive. Think today about those whom you did not forgive, or against whom you are still holding grudges in your heart. Think about it and say, "How can I be in church celebrating today while I have not forgiven others, while I hold grudges against others, while I am saying, 'God forgive me my trespasses as I forgive those who trespass against me'?" Am I lying to God? If you want to carry your cross today—now—raise your heart and ask God to help you forgive all those whom you could not forgive before.

Forgiveness is a very important element in our lives, to the extent that I can say that those who live without forgiveness live a miserable life. All of us, without exception, sin. And because we sin, all of us, without exception, hurt others, either intentionally or unintentionally. And since we are living with human beings, then all of us have also been hurt by others, whether intentionally or unintentionally. So to live together in peace, we need to forgive one another, because I sin against you, and you sin against me. So I need to forgive you, and you need to forgive me.

When couples come to me asking for advice for their marriage, I tell them, "Forgiveness. In your marital life, you will sin against each other, and you will hurt each other unintentionally, or even intentionally." We need to forgive one another, because without forgiveness, our lives will be filled with conflict, fighting, with no peace at all.

Why do I Need to Forgive?

God, in many commandments, asks us to forgive limitless times. When Peter asked Him, "Lord, how often shall my brother sin against me, and I forgive him? Up to seven times?"[69] The Lord said to him, "I do not say to you, up to seven times, but up to seventy times seven."[70] Why does God want me to forgive?

Forgiveness is in my favor, not in the favor of others. Forgiveness is a very important element in healing, in healing my soul. And I will have peace with myself and with God. Even in secular non-Christian counseling, of people who do not believe in God, they speak about forgiveness, because forgiveness means to let go of the debt. When the Lord Jesus Christ explained forgiveness, He explained it as a debt that is forgiven. In the parable from the gospel of Luke, we read in the second watch of Midnight Hour, when Simon judged the Lord because He had accepted the sinful woman and allowed her to wash His feet with her tears, the Lord asked Simon:

---

69 Matthew 18:21.
70 Matthew 18:22.

And Jesus answered and said to him, "Simon, I have something to say to you." So he said, "Teacher, say it." "There was a certain creditor who had two debtors. One owed five hundred denarii, and the other fifty. And when they had nothing with which to repay, he freely forgave them both. Tell Me, therefore, which of them will love him more?"[71]

Let me differentiate between three things: healing, forgiveness, and reconciliation. Let us assume that somebody borrowed $1,000 from me, and they did not pay me back. Forgiveness is to let go of this debt, to forget it, to expect nothing back. For as long as I am expecting this person to pay me back, I will be bothered, angry, and frustrated. I may say, "How come they took this money from me and did not pay me back?" But once I let go of the debt and say, "You know what? Okay, I will forget it," then I will have peace. That is why when we say forgive and forget, it is so that you may have peace in your heart, for your heart to be healed. This is an essential element in healing if you want to be healed.

But if you do not want to be healed, you will go through the negative cycle of lack of forgiveness. Even in the Divine Liturgy, we speak about "the remembrance of vice bearing death."[72] When I remember how people hurt me, it is as if I have a wound and I am opening this wound again and again.

---

71 Luke 7:41–43.

72 The Divine Liturgy of St. Basil – Prayer of Reconciliation.

Every time the wound wants to heal, I am opening it again, so healing will never happen. That is why I say forgiveness is in my favor, for this wound to be healed. For example, when I lent this person $1,000, and they did not pay me back, they hurt me financially. How to cope with this hurt, how to compensate for this loss, that is healing. So when somebody hurts me, how to cope and how to compensate, and how to survive, that is healing. But you cannot be healed without forgiveness.

Reconciliation is another element. Should I lend him money again or not? That is reconciliation. Sometimes we confuse these three things together: forgiveness, healing, and reconciliation. So, why do I forgive others? Because forgiveness gives me healing, peace with myself and also with God. When I choose not to forgive, then I will hold negative feelings inside my heart, and I will go into a vicious cycle. What is this cycle? Hurt causes wounds. When somebody hurts me, they wound me. With any wound, there is pain. If I choose at this moment to forgive and forget, I will be healed. Then the rest of the cycle will be interrupted here. But if I do not choose to forgive, what will happen? Then, with this pain, I will feel the unfairness. How can they take $1,000 from me and not pay me back? This is unfair. Once I start thinking that this is unfair, I will be angry. This anger will start to rise in my heart. Anger leads to what we call bitterness. I feel bitter from inside; I am not happy. Bitterness will lead to hatred. I hate the person who did this to me. Hatred leads to revenge.

I need to take vengeance on this person. Although God said, "Vengeance is mine,"[73] I now want to take revenge. I take the position of God. Then this desire to avenge will turn into an actual act of revenge. So when I take vengeance on others, I hurt them, and because I hurt them, this will cause wounds, pain, unfairness, anger, bitterness, hatred, desire to revenge, revenge, and another wound. And I will hurt them, and they will hurt me. This cycle continues.

And if we look at this cycle, we will find there is anger; anger does not do the will of God. As St. James said, "The wrath of man does not produce the righteousness of God."[74] As for bitterness, it is the opposite of joy. Think about a time in your life in which you did not forget, nor forgive somebody. Think about this time, how angry you were, how you were bitter from inside, how you were not joyful, how you started to hate this person. And the Bible tells us that if, because of anger, you hate somebody, you will be judged just as someone who has committed murder,[75] like Cain, who hated and murdered his brother. And this will lead to revenge and repaying evil for evil, although the Scripture said, "Repay no one evil for evil."[76]

Some of us may justify this and say, "No, I have forgiven, but I am doing what is right," or "I am

---

73 Deuteronomy 32:35.
74 James 1:20.
75 Cf. Matthew 5:21–22.
76 Romans 12:17.

seeking justice," or any other justification. But if you want to know for sure whether you have forgiven or not, examine yourself. Are you healed? If you are still angry, do not deceive yourself. Do not say, "I have forgiven," because if you have forgiven, you will not be angry. If you still have bitterness and are lacking joy, then do not say, "I have forgiven." Forgiveness will bring you peace. Forgiveness will bring you healing. So do not deceive yourself. I will continue to bleed and to walk in darkness, the darkness of hatred and bitterness. And in this way, I will never enjoy or experience the forgiveness of God toward me, although it is available. I will not be able to see it because now I am blind with all these negative emotions. That is why I said that when we decide to forgive, we do it for ourselves, not for the other.

How do I Forgive Others?

Yes, I want to forgive. I know God asked me to forgive, but I cannot forgive. I have the desire, but I cannot forgive. So how can I forgive others?

1. Meditate on How Christ Forgave You

I need to meditate on the forgiveness of Christ to me, and to really understand this forgiveness, and how God loved me and forgave me this huge debt. In prayer, you ask God to forgive you, and then you go and confess your sins. And whatever your sins are, you hear at the end, "May the Lord absolve you." You are forgiven. The sentence of death that you deserve is now removed. You are free. You are righteous before God. How come? Because our beloved Lord Jesus Christ paid the debt for you. He died on the cross to forgive us our sins.

Once, they brought to the Lord Jesus Christ a paralytic man, and it was very difficult to get him through the door. So they made an opening in the ceiling and let this man with his bed down before the Lord Jesus Christ. And everybody was expecting a miracle of healing. So the Lord looked at him and told him, "Your sins are forgiven you."[77] And I can feel the disappointment of everyone. We labored and toiled to carry this person with his bed, and broke through the roof, making an opening, and then we let him down, for You to heal him, and then You tell him, "Your sins are forgiven"? So the Lord asked them a question, "Which is easier, to say to the paralytic, 'Your sins are forgiven you,' or to say, 'Arise, take up your bed and walk'?"[78] At first glance, we may say, "Of course, it is easy to tell him, 'Your sins are forgiven.' These are just words. But to tell him, 'Rise. Carry your bed and walk,' this is a miracle." But this is a wrong answer, because to tell him, "Your sins are forgiven," means the Lord Jesus Christ became man, was born in a manger, was persecuted, attacked, cursed, and at the end of His life, He was crucified.

---

77 Mark 2:5.
78 Mark 2:9.

For your sins to be forgiven, there is a price. St. Peter says, "You were not redeemed with corruptible things, like silver or gold, from your aimless conduct received by tradition from your fathers, but with the precious blood of Christ, as of a lamb without blemish and without spot."[79] Every time you hear, "Your sins are forgiven," know that there is a price paid, the blood of our Lord Jesus Christ. But to tell him, "Rise. Carry up your bed and walk," did not cost the Lord Jesus Christ anything. By the power of His divinity, He can heal him. But some people said, "How could we know that when You told him, 'Your sins are forgiven,' that indeed his sins were forgiven? These are just words." So the Lord told them, "But that you may know that the Son of Man has power on earth to forgive sins,"[80] and then He looked at the man and said to him, "I say to you, arise, take up your bed, and go to your house."[81] Then he rose, carried his bed, and walked. So He did the miracle to prove His authority to forgive sins.

So do you want to forgive your brother? Remember how much the Lord paid for you to be forgiven, to deliver you from the sentence of death, to deliver you from hell, because if He did not save us, this would be the fate of all of us. But He saved us freely. What did we do to deserve this? He saved us freely, without even reprimanding us. The sinful woman in the house of Simon, He did not reprimand her. The thief on the

---

79 1 Peter 1:18–19.
80 Mark 2:10.
81 Mark 2:11.

cross, He did not reprimand him. Zacchaeus, He did not reprimand him. Matthew, the tax collector, He did not reprimand him. The woman who was caught in the act, He defended her, and He looked at everyone and told them, "He who is without sin among you, let him throw a stone at her first."[82] But, unfortunately, we often have beams in our eyes, yet we try to remove the speck from our brother's eyes.

Also, Peter asked this question to the Lord Jesus Christ, "Lord, how often shall my brother sin against me, and I forgive him? Up to seven times?"[83] And the Lord said to him, "I do not say to you, up to seven times, but up to seventy times seven."[84] I am sure that St. Peter's facial expression expressed that this is impossible. How will I be able to forgive my brother 490 times? And by the way, seven multiplied by seventy means unlimited times and unconditional. So the Lord, when he saw the expression on St. Peter's face, gave them a parable, which goes as follows, but I will change the currency to US dollars, in order to understand the concept of forgiveness.

So the Lord said, "The kingdom of heaven is like a certain king."[85] This is God, who wanted to settle accounts with his servants, that is, us. And when he had begun to settle accounts, one was brought to him who owed him 10,000 talents. A talent equals 6,000

---

82 John 8:7.

83 Matthew 18:21.

84 Matthew 18:22.

85 Matthew 18:23.

denarii. And one denarius is a day's wage of a worker. In the parable of the eleventh hour, the Scripture says, "When he had agreed with the laborers for a denarius a day, he sent them into his vineyard."[86] So, how much is the wage of a worker today? Let us assume, for example, $50. So one talent equals 6,000 denarii. So multiplying 6,000 by $50, one talent equals $300,000. And the debt here was 10,000 talents, so this equals three billion dollars. This man is a worker, a servant. How much does he make? If he makes $50 a day and works 350 days, for example,—of course, he works less than this if you consider all the vacations—his annual income is about $18,000. Can a person who makes $18,000 a year pay a debt of $3 billion in any way? It is impossible. Which means, it is impossible to pay our debt to God. That is why Christ came and died on the cross, to pay all our debts.

But as the servant was not able to pay, his master commanded that he be sold. We say in the Divine Liturgy, "We were bound and sold on account of our sins."[87] This means that we sold ourselves to Satan to be in the kingdom of darkness because of our sins. Not only was the servant commanded to be sold, but also his wife and children—Adam, Eve, and all their children—and all that he had, and that payment be made. Of course, we cannot pay this payment. That is why all of us were under the sentence of death. The servant, therefore, fell before him saying, "Master, have

---

86 Matthew 20:2.
87 The Divine Liturgy of St. Basil – Holy.

patience with me, and I will pay you all."[88] Then the master of that servant was moved with compassion, released him, and forgave him the debt. He told him, "You know what? Your debt of $3 billion is forgiven." We pray in the Sixth Hour of the Agpeya, "Tear the handwriting of our sins, O Christ our God," as if there were a promissory note with $3,000,000,000 that we needed to pay. So God took this note, tore it, and threw it away, saying, "You are free. Go. You are forgiven." This is what He did on the cross for each one of us.

But that servant went out and found one of his fellow servants who owed him 100 denarii, which, as we said, equals $5,000. If he makes $18,000 a year, then he can pay the $5,000. And he laid hands on him. I want you to notice that the master did not lay hands on the servant. But the servant laid hands on his fellow servant, and took him by the throat. This is violence and a desire for revenge. You can see here the negative cycle: anger, bitterness, revenge, murder. And he said, "Pay me what you owe." So his fellow servant did exactly what this servant did with the master: He fell at his feet and begged him, saying, "Have patience with me and I will pay you all." And he would not, but went and threw him in prison, till he should pay the debt. This is the prison of avoidance, the prison of slander, the prison of character assassination, the prison of gossiping about him. There are many prisons we can put these people in.

---

88   Matthew 18:26.

So his fellow servants saw what had been done. Who are the fellow servants? Here, the angels because they are the servants of God. And they are in charge of reporting to God our daily conduct. So they reported—that is, the angels—to God what had been done. And the servants were very grieved by the harshness of the heart of this man, and came and told their master all that had been done. Then his master, after he had called for him, said to him, "You wicked servant." So, lack of forgiveness is wickedness. "You wicked servant, I forgave you all that debt, $3 billion, because you begged me. Should you not also have had compassion on your fellow servant for this $5,000 just as I had pity on you?" So, lack of forgiveness is wickedness and also a lack of love. He did not have compassion.

And his master was angry, and delivered him to the torturers until he should pay all that he owed. What are the torturers? It is that negative cycle that I told you. It is the torturer of anger, the torturer of bitterness, the torturer of desire for revenge, because all these feelings will torture the person. And then the Lord concluded by saying, "So My heavenly Father also will do to you if each of you, from his heart, does not forgive his brother his trespasses."[89]

---

89   Matthew 18:35.

The Ineffable Forgiveness of God

2. Choose Between Mercy and Judgment

The Lord taught us clearly, saying, "With the measure you use, it will be measured back to you."[90] So if you choose not to forgive, then with the same measure, it will be measured to you, and you will not be forgiven. Why will we not be forgiven? Because of your lack of forgiveness, you became blind spiritually, and you will not see the forgiveness of Christ that is present and accessible to you. You will not be able to see it and enjoy it, and be forgiven. So you have a choice, to choose between mercy and judgment: mercy, as the Lord has said, "Blessed are the merciful, for they shall obtain mercy,"[91] or judgment and condemnation, "With the measure you use, it will be measured back to you."[92] It is your choice.

How do I Know that I Forgave?

Many people say, "Yes, I forgive him. Yes, I forgive him." There are external and internal signs to help you know whether you have forgiven or not.

The External Signs

The Lord gave us three signs. The first sign is: "Bless those who curse you."[93] Can you bless them? If you are

---

90 Matthew 7:2.
91 Matthew 5:7.
92 Matthew 7:2.
93 Matthew 5:44.

not able to bless those who hurt you, then you have not forgiven them. If you forgive them, you will be able to bless them. The Lord Jesus Christ prayed and said, "Father, forgive them."[94] St. Stephen prayed for the people and said, "Lord, do not charge them with this sin."[95] This is the first external sign: to bless those who curse you. Are you able to bless them?

The second sign is: "Do good to those who hate you."[96] Are you able to do good to them? If they need you, are you able to do good to them?

The third sign is: "Pray for those who spitefully use you and persecute you."[97] Do you pray for them? If you say, "No, I cannot pray for them. I cannot do good to them. I cannot bless them," then you have not forgiven them. What you should do is ask God to help you. Tell Him, "God, I want to forgive, but I cannot. I am still weak. I am here to ask You to grant me Your grace to be able to forgive."

The Internal Signs

I have already said it: Do you have peace with yourself? Are you still angry? Is there bitterness? Is there a desire for revenge? Is there hatred? All these signs tell you that you have not forgiven. Some people forgave and were healed, and then they enjoyed the peace in

---

94 Luke 23:34.
95 Acts 7:60
96 Matthew 5:44.
97 Ibid.

The Ineffable Forgiveness of God

their hearts. Then somebody came with a knife and reopened the wounds. This is the remembrance of evil entailing death. And many times, Satan will deceive these people and say, "You are reopening the wounds for good reason, to clean them more." And then we start to leave this wound to bleed and bleed. In order for these people to be healed, they need to remember the concept of forgiveness. There is no healing without forgiveness. When you remember a certain person in your life who hurt you, even a long time ago, and you are still angry, you hate them, you are not at peace, then you have not forgiven. If you cannot forgive, then ask God to help you. Tell Him, "God, I am weak. I cannot forgive them."

Upon remembering the cross of Christ, ask God to help you with forgiveness, because unlimited, unconditional forgiveness was accomplished on the cross, the forgiveness of the Creator toward us. Not the forgiveness of a servant to another servant, no, rather, the Creator, the God of all of us, forgave us. He carried our iniquities. He stood in front of the Father as a sinner. So did St. Paul say. He became sin[98] and a curse.[99] He stood before the Father instead of me, and He carried the wages of sin that I deserve. He did not have to do all this, but He did it because He loves us. He did not have anger or bitterness; nor did He do this to have peace with Himself. So I marvel that God, who did not need forgiveness and did not need to forgive us

---

98 See 2 Corinthians 5:21.
99 See Galatians 3:13.

to be at peace and joyful, forgave us because He loves us. And we, who need forgiveness for our healing, for our peace, for our joy, refuse to forgive one another. So if there is a lesson we need to learn from the cross, let us think about how much God forgives us and how we ought to forgive one another.

> *"You receive now remission of your sins, and the gifts of the King's spiritual bounty; when war shall come, strive nobly for your King. Jesus, the Sinless, was crucified for you; and will you not be crucified for Him who was crucified for you? You are not bestowing a favor, for you have first received; but you are returning a favor, repaying your debt to Him who was crucified for you in Golgotha."*
>
> **St. Cyril of Jerusalem**
>
> *The Catechetical Lectures* XIII.23. (NPNF[2] 7)

6

Meditations on the Cross

1. My Value to God.

Knowing that you were not redeemed with corruptible things, like silver or gold, from your aimless conduct received by tradition from your fathers, but with the precious blood of Christ, as of a lamb without blemish and without spot.[100]

When we look at the cross, we see our priceless value in the eyes of God. Because our Lord Jesus Christ has paid a very costly price, His body and blood, to redeem us, we are very precious in the eyes of our Lord. Knowing that, we should have no worries about anything in the world. St. Paul says, "He who did not spare His own Son, but delivered Him up for

---

100 1 Peter 1:18–19.

us all, how shall He not with Him also freely give us all things?"[101]

Realizing the value of the human being in the eyes of God, servants and clergy are to be filled with holy love for them, zeal and desire to search for the lost sheep with patience and persistence, and work hard toward the salvation of everyone.

2. The Cross is the Greatest Motive to Consecrate Yourself to God

In his first epistle to the Corinthians, St. Paul says, "Or do you not know that your body is the temple of the Holy Spirit who is in you, whom you have from God, and you are not your own?"[102] How did we obtain the Holy Spirit? How did we become the temple of God? St. Paul explains, saying, "For you were bought at a price; therefore glorify God in your body and in your spirit, which are God's."[103] What is the price? His blood on the cross. If I understand the mystery of the cross, if I understand that I was condemned to death, but the Lord Jesus Christ redeemed me, purchased me, then I am not my own. My life that I am living is not mine, because I was condemned to death. As St. Paul said, "It is no longer I who live, but Christ lives in me."[104] Then I should glorify God in my body and my spirit, because I was bought at a price.

---

101 Romans 8:32.
102 1 Corinthians 6:19.
103 1 Corinthians 6:20.
104 Galatians 2:20.

Why do people not consecrate their lives to God? Because they do not understand the mystery of the cross. They think that they own their lives. They do not know that they do not own their lives. Their lives belong to Him who died for them and purchased them and saved them from the sentence of death. In his second epistle to the Corinthians, St. Paul says, "For the love of Christ compels us, because we judge thus: that if One died for all, then all died."[105] When I think about His love, there being no greater love than this, I feel that I am compelled. Compelled to do what? To live for Him. St. Paul continues, saying, "And He died for all, that those who live should live no longer for themselves, but for Him who died for them and rose again."[106]

St. Paul explains that if you understand the mystery of the cross, the love of Jesus Christ on the cross by shedding His blood for us, if you understand this, then you are compelled, compelled out of love, not out of oppression. Compelled to do what? To live, "that those who live should live no longer for themselves, but for Him." You are compelled by the love of the Lord Jesus Christ. This is why St. Paul, when he understood the love of Christ, consecrated himself completely to the ministry of God.

In the Old Testament, when Moses consecrated Aaron as high priest and his children as priests, he killed

---

105 2 Corinthians 5:14.
106 2 Corinthians 5:15.

a sacrifice, and then he took the blood of the sacrifice and put it on the ear and on the thumb and on the big toe. Why the ear and the thumb and the big toe? From now on, my ear will not listen to anything except the voice of God. My hand will not do anything except the service of God. And my feet will not walk in any way except the way of God. That is the consecration. So, when we understand the mystery of the cross, then it is a big motive for us to consecrate our bodies, our souls, and our lives for Him who died for us.

3. The Cross is Our Strength in Times of Hardship and Tribulation

The cross is also the secret behind enduring hardships, sufferings, pain, and persecution. From the cross, we obtain our strength, the power of God, and the wisdom of God. When we are persecuted, if we carry the cross of Christ in our hearts, then we will welcome the persecution and will be able to endure the suffering, pain, and hardships. Why? Because we are not looking at the suffering, but we are looking forward to the glory that comes after the suffering. As St. Paul said, "If indeed we suffer with Him, that we may also be glorified together."[107] We do not delight in pain and suffering. Of course not. But we can endure suffering because we look to the glory beyond it.

---

107 Romans 8:17.

After speaking about the heroes of the faith in the eleventh chapter of the epistle to the Hebrews, St. Paul says:

> Therefore we also, since we are surrounded by so great a cloud of witnesses, let us lay aside every weight, and the sin which so easily ensnares us, and let us run with endurance the race that is set before us, looking unto Jesus, the author and finisher of our faith, who for the joy that was set before Him endured the cross, despising the shame, and has sat down at the right hand of the throne of God. For consider Him who endured such hostility from sinners against Himself, lest you become weary and discouraged in your souls.[108]

Many of us complain about how difficult the spiritual way is, but St. Paul is telling us, "Let us run with endurance the race that is set before us." How do I get the power to run with endurance? Where do I get this power from? St. Paul says, "Looking unto Jesus, the author and finisher of our faith." He is the beginning and the end. He, for the joy that was set before Him, endured the cross. Which joy? The joy of our salvation. So, if Jesus rejoices in our salvation, and because of this joy, He endured the cross, how much more should we endure?

---

108 Hebrews 12:1–3.

When you are struggling and are facing hardships and difficulties, consider Him who endured such hostility from sinners against Himself, lest you become weary and discouraged in your souls. If you want to get power and strength, consider Him. Think about His cross. And when you get this strength, then you can resist until bloodshed. For St. Paul continues, saying, "You have not yet resisted to bloodshed, striving against sin."[109] You will get this power, the power to endure from the cross of our Lord Jesus Christ.

St. Peter says something similar: "For what credit is it if, when you are beaten for your faults, you take it patiently? But when you do good and suffer, if you take it patiently, this is commendable before God."[110] St. Peter says that if you did something wrong and were punished, and you endured it, you have no credit, because you received what you deserve. There is no credit here. But when we do good and suffer, many of us cannot accept this. Many of us feel that it is not right, it is not fair to suffer while I am doing good. But St. Peter is telling us that God will praise you for this when you endure and take it patiently if you suffer while you are doing good.

And then St. Peter surprises us with the next verse. He says, "For to this you were called."[111] You were called to suffer while you are doing good. And he continues, saying, "Because Christ also suffered

---

109 Hebrews 12:4.
110 1 Peter 2:20.
111 1 Peter 2:21.

for us, leaving us an example, that you should follow His steps: 'Who committed no sin, nor was deceit found in His mouth'; who, when He was reviled, did not revile in return; when He suffered, He did not threaten, but committed Himself to Him who judges righteously."[112] So we are called to endure suffering, even while we are doing good. How come? That is the power of the cross. That is the example that the Lord Jesus Christ left us.

4. The Vanity of the World.

"But God forbid that I should boast except in the cross of our Lord Jesus Christ, by whom the world has been crucified to me, and I to the world."[113] Every time we look at the cross, we know that we are crucified to the world, and the world to us. In Baptism, which is a fellowship and participation in the crucifixion and death of our Lord, we are buried with our Lord Jesus Christ. Thus, "I have been crucified with Christ; it is no longer I who live, but Christ lives in me; and the life which I now live in the flesh I live by faith in the Son of God, who loved me and gave Himself for me."[114]

If the world is crucified to us, it follows that the world is dead to us, and accordingly, we should not desire anything from the world, and the world would

---

112 1 Peter 2:21–23.
113 Galatians 6:14.
114 Galatians 2:20.

not tempt dead people. The cross reminds us that we died, in Baptism, with our Lord Jesus Christ to live with Him. If we still pursue the pleasures of the world, then we are putting ourselves in a position of enmity to God.

The Holy Scripture says, "Friendship with the world is enmity with God."[115] But those who crucify their desires and passions will live and be glorified eternally with Him. For the Holy Scripture says, "And those who are Christ's have crucified the flesh with its passions and desires."[116] So every time I look at the cross, I forget the vanity of the world and remember that I have died, in Baptism, with our Lord Jesus Christ.

5. The Wickedness of Sin.

> Who Himself bore our sins in His own body on the tree, that we, having died to sins, might live for righteousness—by whose stripes you were healed. For you were like sheep going astray, but have now returned to the Shepherd and Overseer of your souls.[117]

Here, St. Peter says that every time I look at the cross, I remember how wicked sin is, how our Lord Jesus Christ had to suffer, and was crucified because

---

115 James 4:4.
116 Galatians 5:24.
117 1 Peter 2:24–25.

Meditations on the Cross

of my sins. In that sense, we should deal with sin very seriously without compromising or adopting a laid-back attitude toward it. May God who was crucified on the cross for my salvation put His cross in our hearts, so that we can say with St. Paul, "It is no longer I who live, but Christ lives in me."[118]

6. What do I do with the Holy Cross?

When the Lord Jesus Christ was arrested, Pontius Pilate asked the following question, "What then shall I do with Jesus who is called Christ?"[119] And every one of us should ask ourselves this question, "What should I do with Jesus who is called Christ?" After you know the power of His cross, what are you going to do with Jesus, the crucified Jesus?

Let me relate a real story that happened with one of the soldiers who was wounded during the American War. This soldier became very poor. So the American government decided to send him to a shelter. They sent an officer to go to his house to take him to the shelter. When the officer entered the house of this soldier, he found a frame, and when he looked at the frame, he found a check in this frame, and it was a real check. This check had the signature of President Abraham Lincoln, and this check was worth a great amount of money. The officer was surprised. How is it that this soldier is living in poverty while he has a

---
118 Galatians 2:20.
119 Matthew 27:22.

check that can make him very wealthy? So he asked him, "Why did you put this check in a frame?" So the soldier replied and said, "Because it has the real signature of Abraham Lincoln, and I do not want to lose it." So the officer was very surprised, and he told him, "So you have this large sum of money and are living in poverty, because you are just content to look at it every morning while living in this poverty?"

Unfortunately, many of us are doing the same with the cross of the Lord Jesus Christ. We look at it every morning, we hold it in our hand, or we have it as a necklace, and then we do not celebrate and venerate the cross by living the life of the crucified Jesus. We need to live the meaning of the cross. The cross is the foundation of many things; we need to live these things. Otherwise, like this soldier who looked at this check every morning, we look at this cross every morning, but we are not living the life of the crucified Jesus.

> *"Let us, therefore, not be ashamed of the Cross of Christ; but though another hide it, do you openly seal it upon your forehead, that the devils may behold the royal sign and flee trembling far away. Make then this sign at eating and drinking, at sitting, at lying down, at rising up, at speaking, at walking: in a word, at every act."*
>
> ### St. Cyril of Jerusalem
>
> *On the Ten Points of Doctrine* 14. (NPNF² 7)

7

The Cross & the Eucharist

In the Gospel of St. John, the Lord Jesus Christ said, "I am the bread of life. He who comes to Me shall never hunger, and he who believes in Me shall never thirst."[120] In the same chapter, the Lord Jesus Christ spoke in detail about the Eucharist, saying, "For My flesh is food indeed, and My blood is drink indeed.... He who eats this bread will live forever."[121] The question here is: What is the link between the Eucharist and the cross?

In the Book of Leviticus, one of the five sacrifices or offerings that were mentioned is the grain offering, the offering of flour.[122] The five offerings are the burnt offering, the peace offering, the trespass offering, the sin offering, and the grain offering. And in the second chapter of Leviticus, there is emphasis that no leaven

---

120 John 6:35.
121 John 6:55, 57.
122 See Leviticus 2.

must be used. The grain offering should be unleavened bread. And the Church Fathers explained this by saying that the grain offering represents the life of our Lord Jesus Christ. And leaven in the Scripture symbolizes sin. As the Lord said to the disciples, "Beware of the leaven of the Pharisees, which is hypocrisy."[123] And since our Lord Jesus Christ lived His life without sin, He once said to the multitude around Him, "Which of you convicts Me of sin?"[124] That is why this offering should be unleavened bread, because it symbolizes the life of our Lord Jesus Christ, who lived a pure, holy, and godly life. As St. Paul said, "[He] was in all points tempted as we are, yet without sin,"[125] and as we say in the Divine Liturgy of St. Gregory, "[He] resembled us in everything, except sin alone."

In the Eucharist, however, we use leavened bread. This is because the Eucharist does not symbolize the life of our Lord Jesus Christ on earth, but it symbolizes, in particular, His sacrifice on the cross, and since He carried our sins, and He became sin,[126] as St. Paul said; and as St. John the Baptist testified about the Lord Jesus Christ, "Behold! The Lamb of God who takes away the sin of the world!"[127] That is why this offering is offered of leavened bread, because leaven symbolizes sin. So the leaven here symbolizes our sins

---

123 Luke 12:1.
124 John 8:46.
125 Hebrews 4:15.
126 See 2 Corinthians 5:21.
127 John 1:29.

that He carried in His body, and crucified our sins on the cross, and abolished death by His death, and then He rose from the dead.

Now, we can understand the connection between the Eucharist and the cross. The sacrifice of the cross is a sacrifice for our sins. He carried our sins, and He nailed them to the cross. Then He gives us life and resurrection. And this life and resurrection, we receive through Communion, through the Eucharist. So now, it is clear why the Church speaks about the Eucharist when we celebrate the second day of the Feast of the Cross.

Also, concerning the wine that we use, some fathers do not use the word "wine," but they prefer to use words like "grape juice." No, what we use in the Eucharist is not just grape juice, but fermented grape juice. Again, the fermentation symbolizes our sins that our Lord Jesus Christ carried on the cross.

What is the Relationship between the Eucharist and Our Resurrection?

The cross has two sides: the crucifixion and the resurrection. He has to die in order to be raised, and with His resurrection, all of us are raised with Him. And He gives us this resurrection through Communion. That is why He said, "Whoever eats My flesh and drinks My blood has eternal life."[128] Notice that in this

---

128 John 6:54.

chapter of the Gospel of St. John, the phrase, "I will raise him up," was repeated three times. The first time, He said, "This is the will of the Father who sent Me, that of all He has given Me I should lose nothing, but should raise it up at the last day."[129] The second time, He said, "And this is the will of Him who sent Me, that everyone who sees the Son and believes in Him may have everlasting life; and I will raise him up at the last day."[130] And the third time, He said, "No one can come to Me unless the Father who sent Me draws him; and I will raise him up at the last day."[131] So three times did the Lord speak about resurrection: "I will raise him up at the last day." How will this resurrection happen? In the Divine Liturgy, we pray, saying, "For every time you eat of this bread and drink of this cup, you proclaim My Death, confess My Resurrection, and remember Me till I come."[132]

Not only is the body of Christ a living body, but it is also a life-giving flesh. The body of Christ has the power to give life. As we say in the Confession at the end of the Divine Liturgy, "I believe, I believe, I believe, and confess to the last breath that this is the life-giving Flesh." So, when we partake of His Body and His Blood, then the sentence of death, which we fall under because of our sins, will be removed. And we will be raised and receive the power of life.

---

[129] John 6:39.

[130] John 6:40.

[131] John 6:44.

[132] The Divine Liturgy of St. Basil – The Institution Narrative.

The power that raised our Lord Jesus Christ from the dead is the same power that we will receive to be raised from the dead. Here on earth, we will receive the resurrection in our souls and our spirits. But on the last day, the power of the resurrection that lies in us but is dormant—I am speaking regarding our bodies—then in the second coming of Christ, our bodies will be raised, raised in a glorified nature, in a different nature, but with the same body. Yes, it is a different nature, but the same body. And the resurrection is the return of the soul to the body. So the soul will return to this body, and the body will be raised. As St. Paul said, "May your whole spirit, soul, and body be preserved blameless at the coming of our Lord Jesus Christ."[133] So, in the resurrection, we will have body, soul, and spirit. The nature of this body will be changed from a physical and material nature into a spiritual nature, but it is the same body.

The Deep Meaning of "I will Raise Him up"

Now, we will explain the meaning of "I will raise him up," which the Lord said three times. The first time, He speaks about the will of the Father, saying, "This is the will of the Father who sent Me, that of all He has given Me I should lose nothing, but should raise it up at the last day."[134] The will of the Father for us is to be saved. Satan tries to deceive many people and

---

133 1 Thessalonians 5:23.

134 John 6:39.

makes them believe that God is against us, that God is lying in wait to catch us in any word we may say, in any action we may do to punish us. This is completely wrong. If this is the will of the Father, all of us would be under the sentence of death. Why did He send His Son to save us? Why did He send His Son to carry our sins? Why did He send His Son to die on the cross? Do not believe Satan when he tries to deceive you and tells you that the will of the Father is to destroy you.

In the Gospel of St. Matthew, when the Lord separated the sheep from the goat, He put the goats on His left side, symbolizing the wicked people, and the sheep on His right side. He said to the sheep on His right side, "Come, you blessed of My Father, inherit the kingdom prepared for you from the foundation of the world."[135] So God prepared for us heaven, not hell, even before the foundation of the world, even before our creation. But He said to the people on His left side, "Depart from Me, you cursed, into the everlasting fire prepared for the devil and his angels."[136] The lake of fire is not prepared for us. God prepared it for the devil because the devil refuses and rejects any economy of salvation for himself or the fallen angels.

Some people ask, "Why did God not make an economy of salvation for the demons?" Because they will not accept any economy of salvation for themselves, because of their arrogance and pride. This

---

135 Matthew 25:34.
136 Matthew 25:41.

is why Satan convinces some people to be prideful like him, and these people reject the economy of salvation. And because they reject the economy of salvation and choose to be part of the kingdom of the devil, then these people are on the left side of Christ, and they will go with the devil to the lake of fire, which was not prepared for human beings, but prepared for the devil and all his angels. So we need to know that the will of God is our salvation. "This is the will of the Father who sent Me, that of all He has given Me I should lose nothing, but should raise it up at the last day."[137]

And the second time in which He also spoke about the resurrection, He said, "And this is the will of Him who sent Me, that everyone who sees the Son and believes in Him may have everlasting life; and I will raise him up at the last day."[138] So the first time, He explained the will. The second time, He explained how we receive this economy of salvation, this gift of salvation. So His will is that all of us be saved. But how are we saved? He explained, "Everyone who sees the Son and believes in Him may have everlasting life."

The word "sees" does not mean just to see like vision, but the word "to see" here means "to know" the Son, like when the Scripture says, "No one has seen God (the Father) at any time,"[139] meaning "No one has known the Father," because Daniel saw the Father in the Old Testament. Also, St. Stephen and St. John the

---

137 John 6:39.

138 John 6:40.

139 John 1:18. Words in parentheses are added for clarification.

beloved saw the Father. There are several visions in the Scriptures in which people saw the Father. So the verse is not speaking about just seeing the Father with our eyes, but rather "to see" means "to know."

Therefore, to be saved, I need to know the Son and to believe in Him. Many people know the Son; they have heard about Him, so they have some intellectual knowledge of the Son. But to believe in Him means to put all your trust and confidence in the Son, and to live with Him day by day, following His footsteps. As St. Paul said, "I have been crucified with Christ."[140] To believe in the Son means to carry your cross and to follow the Son.

How can I be crucified with Christ? How can I follow His footsteps? We may say that this is difficult. Then, He said for the third time, "I will raise Him up." He spoke about the power that we will receive to help us execute this plan. In the first time, He explained to us the plan of God: He wants us to be saved. In the second time, He explained how we are to be saved: know the Son and believe in Him. In the third time, He told us that we are not alone. God did not tell you, "Go, do it by your own power." But rather it is the power of God that helps us to follow the footsteps of the Son, to be crucified with the Son, to crucify the body, the passions, and the desires, as St. Paul said. This is why He said, "No one can come to Me unless the Father who sent Me draws him; and I will raise

---

140 Galatians 2:20.

him up at the last day."[141] "Draws him" means the power, the power that will help us and support us in our spiritual journey.

Therefore, in these three times, it is not just a vain repetition that Christ said, "I will raise him up." But rather in the first time, He spoke about the will of God. In second time, He spoke about how to execute it: to see and to believe. But perhaps it is difficult. Yes, it is difficult. We cannot do it by ourselves. We need the grace of God. That is why He said, "You are not alone. The Father will draw you. The Father will give you the power. The Father will give you the strength that you need to be crucified with the Son, so you will be glorified with the Son too."

This is the relationship between the Eucharist and the crucifixion. In the Eucharist, we have two aspects. The first is the crucifixion, because it is a sacrifice of the Lord Jesus Christ on the cross. This is why it is leavened bread. And the second aspect is that this is the life-giving Flesh. There is death and resurrection. And in the resurrection, it is the will of God the Father, you need to see and believe in Him to be raised, and you are not alone. The Father will give you the power to be crucified with Christ, so you will be raised with Him.

---

141 John 6:44.

8

The Cross &
the Old Testament Offerings

One of the most interesting and intriguing topics in the Old Testament is the sacrifices or offerings that God the Pantocrator had ordered the Israelites to present to Him, and their direct relation to the grand offering of our Lord Jesus Christ on the cross. The Book of Leviticus deals extensively with this issue. In it, we come across the terms like offering, sacrifice, and oblation (Corban).

Offering is a general term that refers to anything offered to God, whether in worship or only in fulfillment of His command. For example, anise and cumin were to be offered according to God's command and not for the sake of worship.

Sacrifice is the term given to the offering when it involves the shedding of blood.

Oblation is the term given to the offering when no blood shed is involved, but the oblation here is meant for worship only. Corban, which is derived from the verb *kurab*, is also used, and it means "bring to God in worship."

The Book of Leviticus distinguishes five types of sacrificial offerings. Each of which typifies an aspect of the cross. In addition, each sacrifice, along with the accompanying rites (which are typically the same for all types of animals), is a reference to the cross. These five offerings are:

1. The Burnt Offering: It is offered with an animal, a male without blemish. This offering symbolizes the divine aspect of the offering of the cross.

2. The Peace Offering: It is offered with an animal, also, either male or female. This offering symbolizes the human aspect of the cross in the sense that the cross accomplished peace between God and humanity. That is why the offering could be either male or female.

3. The Sin Offering: It is offered with an animal, either male or female.

4. The Trespass Offering: It is offered with an animal, either male or female. This offering is assigned for those who have sinned unintentionally or out of ignorance, or anyone who felt that they were in such a situation that required a sacrifice of that kind.

5. The Grain offering: It is offered with grain or wheat.

This chapter will be concerned with the burnt offering and its symbolic relevance to the cross of our Lord Jesus Christ.

The Nature of the Burnt Offering

When God gave Moses the rites that go with the burnt offering, He took into consideration the economic situation of the people. Thus, a cow was offered only by those who could afford it. Otherwise, a goat, a sheep, or a bird could do. As a matter of fact, the blessed Virgin Mary was among those who had birds for their offerings because that was all that the Mother of God could afford. The Scripture says, "And to offer a sacrifice according to what is said in the law of the Lord, 'A pair of turtledoves or two young pigeons.'"[142]

In all of this, what God was concerned about the most was the amount of love people were ready to put into their offerings to Him. We see this attitude clearly stated in the New Testament. The Lord Jesus Christ praised the widow who had offered the two mites over those who had offered a lot of money. That is because in her two mites she invested much more love than the other rich people who had given much more. Therefore, it is required of us to understand God's

---

142 Luke 2:24.

mind that is set not on the offering as an end in itself, but on the end result that is the amount of love that the offering carries.

St. Paul saw this mind of God best manifested in the behavior of the Galatians, "For I bear you witness that, if possible, you would have plucked out your own eyes and given them to me."[143] Love will not offer just the minimum requirement, but over and above.

Characteristics of the Burnt Offering

Male

> Speak to the children of Israel, and say to them: "When any one of you brings an offering to the Lord, you shall bring your offering of the livestock—of the herd and of the flock. If his offering is a burnt sacrifice of the herd, let him offer a male without blemish; he shall offer it of his own free will at the door of the tabernacle of meeting before the Lord."[144]

The burnt offering must be chosen from male animals only because the burnt sacrifice represents the divine aspect of the cross. "For God so loved the world that He gave His only begotten Son,"[145] and, "And

---
143 Galatians 4:15.
144 Leviticus 1:2–3.
145 John 3:16.

[He] became obedient to the point of death, even the death of the cross."[146] The ultimate obedience and love of the Son to the point of shedding His blood on the wood of the cross was smelled as a sweet aroma that appeased the heart of God. Our Lord Jesus Christ is the bridegroom of the Church. As the Apostle Paul said, "For I have betrothed you to one husband, that I may present you as a chaste virgin to Christ."[147]

The word male also indicates seriousness and courage (manliness). "Watch, stand fast in the faith, be brave, be strong."[148] Here, St. Paul is urging believers, both men and women, to be serious in their spiritual quest. Our Lord was quite serious in His pursuit of our salvation to the point of death, the death on the cross, "for this purpose I came to this hour."[149] The cross was His clear goal, and He went to it in manliness. This is why He rebuked Peter harshly when he tried to stand between Him and the cross, saying to him, "Get behind Me, Satan! You are an offense to Me, for you are not mindful of the things of God, but the things of men."[150]

A male sacrifice, therefore, represents our Lord Jesus Christ, the bridegroom of the Church, and the seriousness of the spiritual life.

---

146 Philippians 2:8.
147 2 Corinthians 11:2.
148 1 Corinthians 16:13.
149 John 12:27.
150 Matthew 16:23.

Without blemish

The Burnt Offering represents the Lord Jesus Christ, the Holy One who is without sin. That is why it must be without blemish. He testified of Himself by saying, "Which of you convicts Me of sin?"[151] St. Peter says, "Knowing that you were not redeemed with corruptible things, like silver or gold, from your aimless conduct received by tradition from your fathers, but with the precious blood of Christ, as of a lamb without blemish and without spot."[152]

He is a Lamb without blemish and without spot as St. Paul said, "For such a High Priest was fitting for us, who is holy, harmless, undefiled, separate from sinners, and has become higher than the heavens; who does not need daily, as those high priests, to offer up sacrifices, first for His own sins and then for the people's, for this He did once for all when He offered up Himself."[153]

So the lamb without blemish symbolizes the Lord Jesus Christ who is without blemish. When one of the servants of the High Priest struck the Lord Jesus Christ, our Lord replied, "If I have spoken evil, bear witness of the evil; but if well, why do you strike Me?"[154] This might be misinterpreted by some as being contradictory to the Lord's teaching of turning the other cheek: "Whoever slaps you on your right

---

151 John 8:46.
152 1 Peter 1:18–19.
153 Hebrews 7:26–27.
154 John 18:23.

cheek, turn the other to him also."[155] However, under the circumstances in which these words of our Lord were said, we find Him defending His divinity as being without blemish. Thus, our Lord proves that He is innocent, without blemish, an acceptable sacrifice (on the cross).

On the other hand, when Pontius Pilate sent him to the soldiers, where he was struck and mocked, He did not reply at all. In the Gospel of St. Matthew, the Scripture says, "Then they spat in His face and beat Him; and others struck Him with the palms of their hands, saying, 'Prophesy to us, Christ! Who is the one who struck You?'"[156] Also, in the Gospel of St. Luke, it says, "And having blindfolded Him, they struck Him on the face and asked Him, saying, 'Prophesy! Who is the one who struck You?'"[157]

The difference between the two situations is that, in the first case, before the high priest, He was being blamed for wrong, but in the second case, before Pontius Pilate, it was only a matter of shame and mockery.

Perfect Offering

"He shall offer it of his own free will at the door of the tabernacle of meeting before the Lord."[158]

---

155 Matthew 5:39.
156 Matthew 26:67–68.
157 Luke 22:64.
158 Leviticus 1:3.

the Old Testament Offerings

The explanation for this is that when a person entered the front door of the tabernacle, the first thing he would meet would be the altar of the burnt sacrifice. The person would offer his lamb (or another animal) at the door of the tabernacle, so that the priests could examine it. If it is acceptable, they would enter the tabernacle and offer it on the altar. But if not approved, the offering would not enter the tabernacle. This is why God strictly rebuked the priests of the Old Testament, because they became slack and began accepting imperfect sacrifices to offer to Him.

In the Book of Malachi, He says:

A son honors his father, and a servant his master. If then I am the Father, where is My honor? And if I am a Master, where is My reverence? Says the LORD of hosts to you priests who despise My name. Yet you say, "In what way have we despised Your name?" You offer defiled food on My altar, But say, "In what way have we defiled You?"[159]

What God the Pantocrator wants to convey here is that we are despising His name by offering the blind or lame on His altar. Then God tells them in the same Book:

"You also say, 'Oh, what a weariness!' And you sneer at it," says the LORD of hosts. "And you

---
159 Malachi 1:6–7.

bring the stolen, the lame, and the sick; thus you bring an offering! Should I accept this from your hand?" says the Lord. "But cursed be the deceiver who has in his flock a male, and takes a vow, but sacrifices to the Lord what is blemished—for I am a great King," says the Lord of hosts, "And My name is to be feared among the nations."[160]

These words are harsh words that should make us stop and reflect on the quality of our offerings to God, be it our time, strength, or energy. Do we offer God our best time? Our strength, do we offer the best of it? When we give someone a gift, we endeavor to give them the best. But when you offer to the Lord's brothers (the needy), what do we give? Do we give old things? We tend to give our old things to the Church, for example, an old desk, old clothes, old furniture, and so on.

In the Book of Malachi, there is a conscience-shaking verse that says, "But cursed be the deceiver who has in his flock a male, and takes a vow, but sacrifices to the Lord what is blemished."[161] It says that when someone has something good, but gives God what is less, he is cursed. This goes to show us how much more God is concerned with the quality of the offering than with the type of the offering. If you have a good offering, but give God what is blemished, He is grieved because He takes it as contempt for His name.

---

160 Malachi 1:13–14.
161 Malachi 1:14.

the Old Testament Offerings

Let us tie this burnt offering with the sacrifice of the cross. St. Paul says in the epistle to the Hebrews that He "suffered outside the gate."[162] In the same manner, as the burnt sacrifice was examined before the gate, so was He examined before Herod and Pilate. Then He was offered up upon the altar of the cross. As it says in the Gospel of St. Luke: "Having examined Him in your presence, I have found no fault in this Man."[163] This was a fulfillment of the Old Testament examination of the sacrifice to see if it was without blemish, to be offered on the altar.

In yelling, "Crucify Him, crucify Him,"[164] none of the Jews knew that they were applying the Law, and unknowingly they confirmed that He is an acceptable sacrifice. Just as in the Old Testament, after the priests found the sacrifice without blemish, they brought it in to be offered on the altar; so was He examined, found without blemish, and then taken to the cross.

During the Divine Liturgy, which is the sacrifice of the cross, just as the lamb was brought before the door of the tabernacle, the oblations (offerings) are presented to the priest, to be examined before the door of the altar. So the priest, along with the deacons, examine the loaf of bread (lamb) and wine. The deacons then declare them good and precious (without blemish). Then and only then, and once approved, are they to be brought inside the altar. That is why it

---
162 Hebrews 13:12.
163 Luke 23:14.
164 Luke 23:21.

is wrong to bring the oblations inside the sanctuary before examining them. It is also wrong to store the wine inside the sanctuary. The oblations should not enter the altar except after the examination process.

During the examination process, the people say, "Lord, have mercy," forty-one times, representing the scourging of our Lord. This is because just as our Lord was examined with whips, so the Church examines the oblations by proclaiming, "Lord, have mercy."

Putting the Hand upon the Sacrifice

> Then he shall put his hand on the head of the burnt offering, and it will be accepted on his behalf to make atonement for him.[165]

1. It is identification with the sacrifice, attesting to the fact that, just as this lamb is about to die, so does the person offering it deserve this sentence of death.

2. It is a transferring of the sins from the person to the sacrifice; the sacrifice becomes a replacement or substitution for the person. So when its blood is shed, it is proof that the redemptive work has been done on my behalf.

3. It confirms the punishment of sin being death.

In the Book of Isaiah, the Scripture says, "And

---

165 Leviticus 1:4.

the LORD has laid on Him the iniquity of us all."[166] And also St. Paul says, "For He made Him who knew no sin to be sin for us, that we might become the righteousness of God in Him."[167] In the same way, just as the person became one with the sacrifice by placing his hand upon its head, so did the Lord Jesus become one with us through His incarnation. And in His body we were all represented. This sacrifice was a redemptive sacrifice for us all, through the body of our Lord Jesus Christ on the cross.

In the Divine Liturgy, this is clearly represented. When the priest chooses the bread, he places his hand on it, praying on behalf of all believers. "Remember, O Lord, Your orthodox Christian servants, each one by his name and each one by her name." Then he prays for his family and those who ask to be prayed for. So those who want to put prayer requests on the altar ought to offer them before the examination of the Lamb so that the Lamb (sacrifice) will be offered for them.

After the priest remembers everyone, he finally remembers himself. In so doing, the Church teaches him humility that he should come last.

---

166 Isaiah 53:6.
167 2 Corinthians 5:21.

The Sprinkling of the Blood

"The priests, Aaron's sons, shall bring the blood and sprinkle the blood all around on the altar."[168] This is a symbol that this sacrifice is killed for the whole world. It is sprinkled in a circle, to show that there is no limit to its redemptive work. Likewise, the sacrifice of our Lord Jesus Christ has no limit. It is offered for all sins, all people, for all ages. In the Divine Liturgy, after the examination process, the priest takes the Lamb and goes around the altar in a circle.

The Giving of the Skin to the Priests

"And he shall skin the burnt offering and cut it into its pieces."[169] This shows us that the first sacrifice offered was that of Adam and Eve, because we read in the Book of Genesis that God clothed them in skins. How? "Also for Adam and his wife the LORD God made tunics of skin, and clothed them."[170] And from where did God get the skin? It is obvious that they had offered a sacrifice of animals, and God used this skin for their covering. This is why God was disappointed with Cain, who offered a bloodless sacrifice, for "without shedding of blood there is no remission."[171] So God refused his sacrifice.

The skin was given to the priests, symbolically. In the New Testament, the skin stands for the work of the

---

168 Leviticus 1:5.
169 Leviticus 1:6.
170 Genesis 3:21.
171 Hebrews 9:22.

priesthood in the forgiveness and covering of sins, that is, through the Mystery of Confession.

Division of the Sacrifice into Four Parts

"The sons of Aaron the priest shall put fire on the altar, and lay the wood in order on the fire."[172] The sacrifice was divided into four parts:

1. The parts of the body, with the heart being the most important organ.
2. Blood representing the soul (sprinkled all around).
3. Head representing the mind (thoughts).
4. Fat representing energy or strength. When you do physical exertion, you burn fat. God is saying that your sacrifice should be offered "with all your heart, with all your soul, with all your mind, and with all your strength."[173]

Sprinkling of the Water

But he shall wash its entrails and its legs with water. And the priest shall burn all on the altar as a burnt sacrifice, an offering made by fire, a sweet aroma to the LORD.[174]

---

172 Leviticus 1:7.
173 Mark 12:30.
174 Leviticus 1:9.

The water symbolizes cleanliness. When a person offers God a sacrifice, he must offer it with a pure heart, just as the Lord is pure from without and within. God is not just concerned with the outward purity. This is why all the inner organs were cleansed with water before being placed upon the altar. It also symbolizes Baptism, which cleanses us from sins. The priest, during the Divine Liturgy, wipes the Lamb with water during the Offering of the Lamb, representing the cleansing of the sacrifice (OT), as well as the baptism of our Lord in the Jordan River (NT).

Thus is the link between the burnt sacrifice and the Divine Liturgy. The sacrifice of the Divine Liturgy is the same as the sacrifice of the cross, as the priest prays in the Confession at the end of the Divine Liturgy, that It is one sacrifice.

Burning the Sacrifice Completely

God commanded that the sacrifice should be burnt completely. This is done in order to show that the Son accepted in full the fire of the divine wrath against sin, drinking the cup of sufferings fully. In Gethsemane, He said, "My soul is exceedingly sorrowful, even to death."[175] And on the cross, He experienced sufferings in their fullness. So, since this burnt sacrifice showed the divine aspect of the cross, it must be burned completely. In addition, our Lord fully surrendered

---

175 Matthew 26:38.

Himself by His own will, as it is mentioned in the Holy Scripture, "of his own free will."[176]

These were the exact rites in which the burnt sacrifice was to be offered to God, an exact prelude and a replica of the burnt offering of the New Testament, our Lord Jesus Christ who offered Himself willingly and obediently as a sweet aroma to God out of His love for mankind, "Christ also has loved us and given Himself for us, an offering and a sacrifice to God for a sweet-smelling aroma."[177]

May God smell in us the sweet aroma of obedience and submission to His will, and that we may love Him and serve Him all the days of our lives on earth.

"While what was upon our Savior appeared to human eyes to be a cross of wood, in the eyes of the Father of all it was really an altar great and lofty, raised up for the salvation of the world and smoking from a sacrifice sacred and all-holy."[178]

St. Cyril of Alexandria

---

176 Leviticus 1:3.

177 Ephesians 5:2.

178 Cyril of Alexandria, *Festal Letters 1–12*, Amidon P.R., trans.; O'Keefe J.J., ed. (Washington, D.C.: The Catholic University of America Press, 2009), 98–99.

Concluding Remarks

The Feast of the Cross may be the only feast that we celebrate twice; besides that, we also commemorate the crucifixion of our Lord Jesus Christ during the Holy Week. The reason why the Church gives the Feast of the Cross this importance and attention is that the cross is the center of Christianity. The cross is the answer to a very important and serious question: How did God save humanity? No other religion has answered this question while remaining faithful to the justice and mercy of God, because where would God's justice be, if God forgave the sins of the people without consequences, since the wages of sin is death? All other religions are a set of morals. But Christianity, because it is the true revelation from God, addressed this serious question of salvation. And the cross became the sign of our discipleship to the Lord. He said, "If anyone desires to come after Me, let him deny himself, and take up his cross, and follow Me."[179] And carrying the cross, not just in the form of holding a cross or wearing a cross, but as He carried the cross for us to save us, we carry the cross for Him.

The cross was a symbol of shame and was a curse. The cross is a symbol of suffering. So to carry the cross means to enter through the narrow gate and to walk in the difficult way willingly. To carry the cross is to accept and to endure suffering for the name of Christ, and to endure the challenges of keeping His commandments,

---

179 Matthew 16:24.

the Old Testament Offerings

and to endure denying yourself the pleasures of the world. The cross is to walk the second mile, which is the mile of love and the mile of sacrifice. As the Lord has said, "And whoever compels you to go one mile, go with him two."[180] Why? Because if I just walk one mile, it may be out of oppression, because I cannot say no. But when I walk willingly the second mile, it is the mile of love toward God and others. When we look at the cross, there are many beautiful meanings in the cross. And to carry the cross in our life means to carry these beautiful virtues in our life. "And as Moses lifted up the serpent in the wilderness, even so must the Son of Man be lifted up, that whoever believes in Him should not perish but have eternal life."[181]

> *"That wood of the cross is, then, as it were a kind of ship of our salvation, our passage, not a punishment, for there is no other salvation but the passage of eternal salvation."*
>
> ## St. Ambrose of Milan
>
> *On the Holy Spirit* I.IX.110. (NPNF² 10)

---

180 Matthew 5:41.
181 John 3:14–15.

"Do you not know what great result the cross has achieved? It has abolished death, has extinguished sin, has made Hades useless, has undone the power of the devil, and is it not worth trusting for the health of the body? It has raised up the whole world, and do you not take courage in it?"

St. John Chrysostom

Instructions to Catechumens 2. (NPNF[1] 9)

www.ingramcontent.com/pod-product-compliance
Lightning Source LLC
Chambersburg PA
CBHW032146040426
42449CB00005B/422